BEYOND
THE WALLS

The Legacy of Humanity

This book is designed to complement the reading experience and bring the reader closer to a work of great impact. This book is not intended to replace the original work, nor does it have the authorization, approval, license or endorsement of the author or publisher of the original work.

Editorial Nova makes no warranties or representations as to the accuracy or completeness of the contents of this book.

All rights reserved, including, without limitation, the right to reproduce this book or any part thereof in any form or by any means, whether electronic, mechanical, or any other means now known or hereafter developed, without the express written permission of the publisher.

BEYOND THE WALLS: THE LEGACY OF HUMANITY
Copyright © 2025 Editorial Nova.
ISBN: 979-8-3485-1468-6

Contents

Introduction
Shiganshina District and the Scout Legion
Training and First Missions
The Fight for Survival: The Power of the Titans
The Expedition and the Female Titan Trap
Annie's Past and the Stohess Investigation
Levi's Past and Infiltration into the Legion
Attack of the Beast Titan and the Crisis in the Legion
The Search for Truth and the Fall of the Government
The Battle at the Chapel and the Transformation of Rod Reiss
The Reign of History and the Discovery of the Ackermans
Grisha 's Basement
The Battle of Shiganshina and the Death of Erwin
The Outside World and the History of Humanity
The Marley Expedition and the World Alliance
Zeke's Plan and Euthanasia for the Eldians
Eren's Internal Conflict and Betrayal
Zeke's Past and His Connection to the Founding Titan
The Activation of the Rumble and Eren's True Will
The Final Fight and the Legacy of the Legion
Ymir's Connection to Eren's Will
Epilogue
Final Note
Curiosities
Legal Notice and Copyright
Disclaimer

Introduction

In a world ravaged by titans, humanity takes refuge behind enormous walls, believing they live in peace. However, this tranquility is an illusion, as the outside is a place full of creatures that devour humans. Within these walls, on the island called Paradis , we meet Eren Yeager, a boy who lives in the Shiganshina district with his sister Mikasa and his friend Armin. Eren's life changes drastically when a colossal titan destroys Wall Maria, allowing the titans to enter and marking the beginning of a nightmare.

Eren, filled with rage and thirst for revenge, decides to join the army, specifically the Scout Legion, a military branch that fights the Titans outside the walls. His goal is clear: to see the outside world and eradicate the Titans, despite the high risk this entails. Alongside him, Mikasa , who instinctively protects him, and Armin, a brilliant strategist, embark on a path of training to become soldiers.

The military is divided into three main branches: the Military Police, who maintain order within the walls; the Garrison Legion, who are tasked with defending the walls; and the Scout Legion, who fight outside of them. Eren, from the start, shows a strong desire to join the Scout Legion, those who directly confront the Titans, despite the high mortality rates.

During their training, Eren and his companions discover that the fight against the Titans is far more complex than they imagined. Titans are not just mindless beasts, but some possess intelligence and even the ability to transform into humans. One of the first mysteries they face is the appearance of a talking Titan who speaks strange words, hinting that there is something more behind these beings. As the story progresses, the Survey Corps actively seeks to understand the origin of the Titans and how to defeat them, leading them to undertake risky expeditions beyond the walls.

Eren, after several incidents, discovers that he also has the power to transform into a titan, which makes him a key piece for the survival of humanity. This ability, far from being a blessing, makes him the object of suspicion and fear by some military personnel and citizens. However, it also becomes a fundamental weapon in the fight against the titans.

The Survey Corps, led by figures such as Erwin Smith and Captain Levi, constantly strive to gain valuable information about the Titans. One of the crucial clues they find is a diary of a female soldier named Ilse, where it is revealed that a Titan spoke to her, uttering the phrase "I am Ymir's servant." These words, along with other discoveries, raise the idea that the Titans have some sort of connection to the past and a figure named Ymir.

Expeditions outside the walls are extremely dangerous and result in heavy casualties. The Scout Legion, despite their losses, continues to search for answers about the origin of the Titans. On one such expedition, they are confronted by a Female Titan, an intelligent being that wreaks havoc among the soldiers. This event leads the Legion to suspect that shifting Titans such as the Colossal Armored Titan, which attacked the Shiganshina district , are among them, infiltrators.

Eren and his companions find themselves embroiled in a conspiracy involving the Military Police and the government. Their main goal is to protect the secrets of the walls and the truth about the Titans, knowledge that is linked to a royal family and a basement in Eren's old home. As the plot progresses, the characters realize that the threat of the Titans is just the tip of the iceberg and that there are darker, more complex forces at work in the shadows.

The mysteries multiply when it is discovered that within the walls, there is a hidden titan, a fact that reveals the manipulation of the government and the royal family. This causes a coup d'état, where the Legion, with the help of other military forces, takes control. Story Reiss, a companion of Eren, is revealed to be a descendant of the royal family, and is the one who must take the throne after the overthrow of the corrupt government.

With the truth revealed, and with the discovery of Eren's basement, the Survey Corps learns about the history of the outside world. They discover that humanity is not extinct outside the walls, and that the Titans are not mindless creatures, but are people of the Eldian race, transformed as a punishment or tool of war. Paradis Island is nothing more than a refuge for the Eldians , considered an evil race and persecuted by the nation of Marley.

The story takes place in Marley, a nation that uses Eldians as tools of war, transforming them into Titans to fight in their battles. The Eldians living in Marley are also persecuted and mistreated, causing a cycle of hatred and revenge between the two nations. Marley's warriors, including Reiner and Bertholdt , who had attacked Paradis , are also victims of this war.

Eren, upon discovering the truth, becomes a radical. Aware of the threat posed by the outside world, he decides to attack Marley, using the power of the Founding Titan. His goal is to protect his people from extinction, even if it means sacrificing other humans. Eren's former allies, including Mikasa and Armin, find themselves at a crossroads, having to choose between their loyalty to Eren or their desire to end the cycle of violence and oppression that has marked their world.

The story culminates in an epic conflict, where the Rumble, the release of thousands of Colossal Titans, is unleashed by Eren to destroy the world's civilization. His former companions, now allied with warriors from Marley, attempt to stop him, understanding the horror of the situation. The final fight is not just against a Colossal Titan, but against a system of hatred and oppression that has been perpetuated through the centuries, where each individual must confront their own morality and the meaning of their actions.

Eren, in his quest for freedom, has become a controversial figure, a villain to some and a hero to others. The story raises questions about the nature of good and evil, justice and revenge, and the responsibility of individual actions in a world marked by violence.

Shiganshina District and the Scout Legion

Shiganshina district , inside Wall Maria, life was relatively normal for Eren Yeager, Mikasa Ackerman, and Armin Arlert . Eren, an impulsive and passionate child, lived with his parents, Carla and Grisha , a quiet life, although often interrupted by his dreams about the outside world. Eren was shown to be a restless and dreamy boy, but with a deep frustration at being locked behind the walls, longing to know what was beyond. His curiosity often led him to question the reality they lived in, wondering what kind of world existed outside the protection of the walls. Mikasa , meanwhile, was Eren's adoptive sister, a young woman of great strength and physical abilities, who was always willing to protect him. Their bond was unbreakable, and her concern for Eren's safety was her priority. Armin, Eren's best friend, was a physically weaker boy, but with a brilliant mind and a great knowledge of the world, thanks to the books he had read. Armin shared Eren's dream of seeing the outside world, and together they imagined what the landscapes and wonders hidden behind the walls would be like.

Eren's longing for the outside world was a constant in his life. This desire was not just a childish curiosity, but a deep need to break away from the monotony and lack of freedom he felt behind the walls. His dream was to explore the vast oceans, frozen lands, and white sand deserts that he imagined existed beyond his reality. His frustration grew when he saw the soldiers of the Survey Corps returning from their expeditions, as he considered them to be humanity's only hope of exploring the outside world.

The return of the Scout Legion to Shiganshina was an event that always marked Eren. Although he viewed them with admiration, the harsh reality of war became evident when observing the small number of soldiers returning, many of them wounded and traumatized. This sight only increased his determination to join the Legion and fight the Titans. The difference between the ideal he had of soldiers and the reality he witnessed led Eren to feel deep frustration, observing how the garrison soldiers were in a state of inactivity and drunkenness.

Driven by this feeling of helplessness and his desire to explore the world, Eren makes the decision to join the Scout Legion, something he tells his parents during a family dinner. His parents' reaction was one of surprise and rejection. Carla, his mother, was very worried and distressed at the idea of her son risking his life on such a dangerous mission. She did not want her son to be part of the Scout Legion and asked him why he had made this decision. Grisha , his father, although less expressive, questioned Eren's motivation, wanting to know why he longed to join the Legion and expose himself to such an uncertain fate. Eren replied that he wanted to see the outside world and that he did not want the lives of soldiers to be in vain, expressing his admiration for the Scout Legion.

During those same days, Mikasa visits Eren in Shiganshina . Her concern for Eren's well-being always kept her close, watching his every move. During the visit, Mikasa accompanied Eren when he decided to defend Armin from a group of kids who were bullying him, demonstrating her strength and ability to protect her friends. Mikasa 's visit to Shiganshina also coincides with the moment when Eren expresses his desire to join the Scout Legion, something she was hearing for the first time.

These early incidents in the lives of Eren, Mikasa , and Armin set the stage for their future, where the quest for freedom, the fight against titans, and the discovery of the truth about the world will become the central axis of their lives. Eren's longing for the outside world, Mikasa 's sense of responsibility , and Armin's intelligence combine to create a trio of characters who will face unimaginable challenges in their fight for survival and truth. Eren's dream of seeing the outside world, initially an innocent aspiration, becomes the driving force behind a series of events that will change the fate of humanity within the walls.

Training and First Missions

After joining the military, Eren, Mikasa , and Armin, along with other recruits such as Jean, Connie, Sasha, Marco, Krista, Ymir, Reiner, Bertolt, and Annie, faced a rigorous three-year training under the supervision of Keith Shadis . This period was filled with physical and mental challenges, designed to prepare the younglings for the harsh realities of fighting the Titans. The recruits were required to master the use of the Three-Dimensional Maneuvering Gear, an essential tool for combating the Titans, as well as learn military tactics and how to work as a team. Eren initially struggled with the equipment, but later discovered that his equipment was defective, managing to improve his skills over time. The training not only tested the recruits' physical abilities, but also their personalities and relationships.

Within this training context, the dynamics between the recruits were complex and contentious. Disputes arose, especially between Eren and Jean, who often clashed due to their different viewpoints and personalities. However, these tensions also allowed bonds and friendships to form, as the recruits learned to trust and support each other in the midst of adversity. The training proved instrumental in building the character and determination of the young soldiers, preparing them for the danger that awaited them.

During a training mission, the squad was split into two groups with the goal of finding an object and returning to base. This training mission turned out to be more complicated than expected, highlighting the importance of coordination and strategy. The first group, led by Marco and with Armin in charge of notes, faced constant fights between Eren and Jean, hindering their progress. The second group, with Thomas and Mikasa , took a different path. The mission served as valuable field experience, revealing the strengths and weaknesses of each recruit and preparing the youngsters for the challenges to come.

The Scout Legion, meanwhile, had as its primary goal to gain information on the Titans, as their origin and motivation were unknown. Squad leader Hanji Zoë insisted on the need to capture Titans for study, though this idea was opposed by Commander Erwin due to a lack of resources and personnel. The pursuit of knowledge about the Titans became a priority for the Legion, recognizing the importance of understanding the enemy in order to effectively combat them.

In the midst of the Legion's investigations, a peculiar incident occurred that raised even more questions about the Titans. A Titan, which was initially pursuing Hanji , suddenly changed course to begin striking a tree. After being shot down by Levi, the tree was found to contain the corpse of a year-old soldier named Ilse, as well as her diary. This discovery proved to be a puzzling and disturbing event for the Legion, as it revealed a strange connection between Titans and humans. Ilse's diary recounted her final moments of life after losing her squad and equipment.

Ilse's journal revealed an even more mysterious encounter: a talking Titan that bowed to her, uttering the words "I am Ymir's servant." This disconcerting behavior suggested a complexity to Titans that the Legion did not yet understand. Though Ilse attempted to communicate with the Titan, it eventually went mad and devoured her. This discovery provided a wealth of information and more questions, prompting Hanji to write a petition for Erwin to allow the capture of Titans for study. The Talking Titan incident and Ilse's journal became a catalyst for research into Titans and the search for answers about their nature, behavior, and origin, further spurring the Survey Legion to understand the mystery surrounding these creatures.

The Fight for Survival: The Power of the Titans

After completing his training, Eren decides to join the Survey Corps, driven by his desire to see the outside world and his thirst for revenge against the Titans who destroyed his home and caused the death of his mother. His determination to wipe out the Titans was strengthened by witnessing the fall of the Shiganshina District , where he experienced the loss and horror of war. Armin and Mikasa , meanwhile, do not hesitate to follow him, also joining the Survey Corps, moved by their loyalty to Eren and their desire to protect him.

In the midst of the chaos caused by the Colossal Titan's attack, Eren accidentally discovers his ability to transform into a titan. This event occurs when, driven by a survival instinct and remembering his father's words, he bites his hand and activates his power. Eren's transformation into a titan was a shocking and confusing event, both for him and his companions, since no one understood the origin of his abilities. This event generated distrust among the soldiers. Upon exiting his titan form, Eren is surrounded by the military who hesitate whether to execute him or not.

In the face of widespread confusion and fear, Armin devises a plan to save Eren and use his power to benefit humanity. Armin attempts to convince the military that Eren is an ally and that his power could be the key to retaking Trost District . Through his persuasion and the intervention of the garrison's leader, Pixis , Eren is able to avoid execution and gains the opportunity to prove his usefulness. Armin's plan was crucial in changing the military's perception of Eren, allowing his power to be seen as a valuable tool in the fight against the Titans.

Eren's ability to transform into a Titan becomes an extremely important asset to humanity. His power, though mysterious and difficult to control, represented a hope to turn the titan threat around. The military recognizes that Eren's power is essential to reclaiming lost territory and to prevent the Titans' advance. Eren's power to regenerate also becomes evident, after recovering from an injury caused by Levi during his trial. He was shown to be able to regenerate lost limbs, such as a leg and an arm.

However, his power also comes with great risk, and so Eren is put on trial where his fate is decided. The choice is between allowing Eren to live and serve humanity or executing him immediately. At this trial, Levi beats Eren to the punch to prove that he can transform whenever he wants and that he is not a threat. Ultimately, it is decided that Eren will be integrated into the Survey Corps, under the supervision of Levi and his squad.

Eren is assigned to Levi's squad, where he bonds with his fellow Titans Auruo , Erd , Gunter, and Petra. They become his mentors and companions, helping him understand his abilities and improve his control as a Titan. Levi's squad, while harsh in their methods, cares for Eren's safety and progress. However, they also have the responsibility of finishing off Eren should he ever lose control of his Titan form. Furthermore, Levi is revealed to be obsessed with cleanliness, leading the entire squad to perform chores at night. During these nights, the squad interacts with Eren as they quietly converse, helping them establish a connection and a sense of camaraderie.

Before their first expedition outside the walls, Commander Erwin gives a speech to the new recruits of the Scout Legion. In this speech, Erwin is completely honest about the difficult situation and high risk involved in fighting the Titans. His goal is that only those who are truly prepared and determined will remain in the Legion. After the speech, many recruits decide to withdraw, leaving only those who were willing to risk their lives for humanity. This speech serves as a filter, ensuring that only the bravest and most committed will become part of the Legion.

The Expedition and the Female Titan Trap

Following Eren's integration into the Scout Legion, a plan was drawn up to retake Wall Maria and the Shiganshina district . The main objective was to discover the secret hidden in the basement of Eren's house, where it was believed that the key to the origin of the Titans was. This plan involved retaking the lost territory and advancing towards the truth about the outside world. Erwin, the commander of the legion, reveals the plan to retake Wall Maria and the Shiganshina district in order to discover the secret that Eren's basement holds. However, this plan also carries a high risk, as they will directly confront the Titans.

In the midst of this preparation for the expedition, it is revealed that Reiner, Bertolt, and Annie, Eren's companions, were the Titans who attacked humanity some years ago. Reiner reveals to Eren that he is the Armored Titan and Bertolt is the Colossal Titan, and that their goal is to exterminate the humans living within the walls. This revelation causes great shock and confusion in Eren and his companions. It is also revealed that Annie is the Female Titan, who is searching for Eren. In the midst of this situation, Eren remembers the moments he spent with Levi's squad and their conversations, leading him to make an important decision on who to trust.

During the expedition, the legion faces a trap set by the Female Titan, an intelligent Titan with superior combat abilities. This Titan surprises everyone with its ferocity, killing several soldiers who cross its path. Armin, observing the Female Titan, realizes that it has its own intelligence and is equal to the Colossal and Armored Titans. Armin understands that there is a human inside the Female

Titan and deduces that its main objective is to find Eren. Thus, Armin, Reiner and Jean try to restrain the Female Titan, but their effort is useless. However, due to Erwin's strategy, the Female Titan is trapped. However, it begins to scream loudly, causing the Titans surrounding them to head towards that place.

Despite the Legion's attempts to capture the Female Titan, Levi's squad is wiped out by it. Petra, one of Eren's companions, is crushed by the Titan, and the other members of the squad are killed trying to stop it. With his squad annihilated, Eren realizes that he made the wrong decision and blames himself for trusting his companions. The death of his companions causes Eren great frustration and rage.

Following the loss of his comrades, Eren transforms into a Titan and decides to fight the Female Titan. The fight is fierce and demonstrates the power of both Titans. However, during the fight, Eren loses control, letting out his rage. Eventually, Levi intervenes and pulls Eren out of the Titan, as it could not devour Annie. The battle ends with the capture of the Female Titan, but at a high price: the loss of Levi's squad. The revelation that Annie is the Female Titan creates even more confusion and distrust among the Legion members. In the end, Ani is caught by the soldiers and Eren begins to attack her relentlessly.

During the battle against the Female Titan, it is discovered that the Female Titan also has the ability to regenerate, just like Eren. This suggests that other Titans may have similar abilities.

Annie's Past and the Stohess Investigation

During a day off before the Legion's expedition, Annie encounters a nightmare in which she relives the battle against Eren and the Legion. This nightmare reminds her of her mission to capture Eren and causes her to reflect on her past and her true goals. Despite being on her day off, Annie decides to don her Military Police uniform, demonstrating her dedication to her duty. She receives a letter from Reiner informing her that he is practicing for the day of the expedition, which serves as a reminder of the mission they must accomplish. At the same time, Hitch comments that she should not wear the uniform on her day off.

Taking advantage of her day off, Annie receives a mission from the Military Police to find a missing girl named Carly Stratmann . This mission is entrusted to her by Hitch in exchange for Annie covering for her on her patrol the next day. Annie accepts the mission, which serves as a distraction from her thoughts and as preparation for her real mission in the legion. Annie obtains information about Carly, a 20-year-old girl, the only daughter of Eliot Stratmann , president of a company called Marlen . The young woman disappeared two days before her father filed the report, which seemed strange to her, since she always had dinner at home.

In her investigation, Annie follows several leads, starting with Carly's father's house. Mr. Stratmann is upset to realize that the Military Police have not done much to find his daughter. Annie manages to get valuable information from Mr. Stratmann , who reveals that his daughter had no friends and was doing nothing after her chemistry studies. Annie then goes to a bar where Carly is known to have used to hang out, where she learns that she was very kind and generous, but that she disappeared 10 days ago after storming out of the place. There she also discovers that Carly was being sought by a dangerous man with prosthetic eyes and a red eye.

Following another lead, Annie finds Carly's boyfriend Kemper's house, a dangerous and hidden area. Upon entering, she finds Kemper's lifeless body under the bed, leading her to conclude that he might be involved in Carly's disappearance. Annie realizes that by failing to find the culprits behind Kemper's death, she herself has become a suspect. However, Annie's priority is to find Carly to prevent her mission in the Legion from being compromised. Annie suspects that Kemper and Carly were selling an illegal substance, which could explain the money Carly had despite her father being broke.

While searching for more clues, Annie is cornered by a red-eyed man named Walt and his men. Walt reveals to Annie that he is also looking for Carly and that he knows that she has not gone to the police base after seeing Kemper's body. In the face of this situation, Annie escapes by using her titan power to destroy the hearse she was being taken to and attacks Walt, who ends up revealing that he was hired by Carly's father. Just as Walt is about to reveal Carly's location, one of his men shoots him, but Annie pretends to be dead so that her attacker will go away. After this, Annie forces Walt to reveal Carly's location.

Annie eventually finds Carly, who reveals that she is the creator of the illegal substance. Carly explains that she created the substance to help her father, who was broke. She also reveals that her father had betrayed the plan, so she storms out of the bar. After a conversation, Carly decides to leave town and Annie gives her a pass to the Rose Wall.

Annie decides to alter her report, saying that Carly and Kemper forged their names and managed to obtain passes to Wall Rose in an unknown way. In this way, Annie is cleared of any suspicion and can focus on her main goal: capturing Eren on the Legion's next expedition. Annie is tired of everything that is happening and does not want to involve anyone in trouble, so she decides to hide the truth. Upon completion of the task, Annie aims to return home to her father, who trained her in hand-to-hand combat. Her greatest desire is to return to her father, who promised her that he would always be with her.

Levi's Past and Infiltration into the Legion

Deep in an underground city, Levi lived a precarious existence alongside his friends, Isabel and Furlan . This place, where sunlight barely penetrated, was their home and refuge. The three shared a life marked by necessity and cunning. Using the three-dimensional maneuvering equipment they had illegally obtained, Levi, Isabel, and Furlan made a living by committing petty thefts and causing disorder in the city. Their skill in using this equipment was such that they had earned a reputation among the inhabitants and local authorities. Levi's life in this underground environment had made him a skilled individual, but it had also marked him with a deep distrust of the outside world.

Levi's life took an unexpected turn when he and Isabel met a group of men who offered them a job. At first, Levi and Furlan were reluctant to get involved, but the promise of being cured and living on the surface as part of the payment convinced them to accept. These men revealed that if they followed their orders, they would be allowed to live on the surface, a longing shared by the three friends. However, the appearance of the Military Police during their first mission made them suspect that the situation might be more complicated than it seemed. The pursuit by the authorities led them to make a risky decision: accept the deal to infiltrate the Scout Legion.

Despite his misgivings, Levi decides to accept the offer to join the Scout Legion as part of a plan that would allow them to live on the surface. This plan involved a deal with a man named Nicholas Lobov , who demanded that they infiltrate the Legion to steal a document from Erwin Smith and kill him. In order not to arouse suspicion, they are told that they must show some resistance before surrendering to the Legion. During this period, Levi, Isabel, and Furlan are introduced as new recruits and undergo harsh training. The addition of these new members causes arguments among some soldiers, but Erwin insists that their skills are of great use to the Legion.

Amidst tensions, Levi and his comrades begin their training in the legion, where their prowess quickly stands out. Despite the doubts of some soldiers, Levi proves to be an exceptional recruit, exceeding everyone's expectations. However, despite his talent and ability, Levi does not lose sight of his initial objective: to infiltrate and complete Lobov 's mission . Meanwhile, Sub-Commander Erwin and Commander Shadis become aware of Lobov 's true plans . Although Lobov believed the mission to be a secret, Erwin was already aware of the infiltration and its objective.

Levi and his companions' real plan was to obtain a document from Erwin and assassinate him outside the walls. However, Levi decides to go on the robbery mission alone, as he considers facing the Titans to be something very dangerous that only he can do. His companions, Isabel and Furlan , do not agree with this decision and argue with him, but after observing the moonlight, Levi decides to trust his friends and take them with him. However, when they venture outside the walls, they face an unexpected situation. A thick fog makes visibility difficult, and in the midst of the confusion, Isabel and Furlan are attacked by a Titan.

Despite his best efforts, Levi witnesses the horrific deaths of his friends, who are devoured by a titan. The loss of Isabel and Furlan unleashes an uncontrollable rage in Levi. In an act of revenge, he attacks the titan in a brutal and bestial way until he finishes it off. However, his revenge does not bring back his friends. After the attack, the other members of the legion realize that Erwin was also in the area and head towards him. At first, Levi decides to confront Erwin, blaming him for the death of his companions, but the commander was already aware of everything that happened, since the document he carried with him was false.

In the midst of his grief and rage, Levi meets Erwin, who reveals that he already knew about Lobov's plan . He also confesses that the document they were trying to steal was fake. Despite having lost his friends and having failed in his mission, Levi decides to follow Erwin's path. Erwin convinces him not to regret his actions, as that would prevent him from making good decisions in the future. Thus, Levi agrees to join the Survey Corps permanently, where he decides to follow his own ideals and see the world through his own eyes, without any regrets for the decisions he makes from now on.

Attack of the Beast Titan and the Crisis in the Legion

The relative calm within the walls was abruptly shattered by the appearance of a terrifying new enemy: the Beast Titan. Unlike any seen before, this Titan not only possessed great strength, but also the ability to think and speak. During an attack on the Legion's troops, the Beast Titan threw a horse at Mike, causing him to fall into the hands of other Titans, who cruelly devoured him at the order of the Beast Titan himself. The death of Mike, one of the Legion's strongest soldiers, demonstrated the threat posed by this new enemy, who seemed to have unusual intellect and cruelty.

As the Legion tried to understand the magnitude of the new threat, another mystery was revealed: the presence of a Titan within Conny's house. This Titan, which seemed to have a connection to Conny's family, raised many questions. Furthermore, it was discovered that the Titans that came from Conny's village bore a strong resemblance to the inhabitants of the place. This revelation led the Legion to suspect that the Titans might be transformed humans, which added further uncertainty to the situation. Amidst this confusion, Hanji discovered that fragments of the walls had the same material as the crystal Annie left behind. This discovery suggested that the Titans within the walls could be functioning as pillars, a theory that Armin had already raised.

Amidst the chaos, Ymir and Historia's secret was revealed, as was their connection to a mysterious Wall Cult. Ymir, who had until then kept her secret, revealed that she also possessed the power to transform into a Titan. In turn, it was discovered that Historia was actually the daughter of the Reiss family, a family with connections to the Wall Cult. At the same time, the Legion also discovered that there was an important person within the Legion that the Wall Cult was keeping an eye on. The cult, led by Pastor Nick, refused to reveal information about the secrets of the Walls and the Titans, causing further suspicion.

As the Legion struggled to unravel the mysteries surrounding it, Reiner and Berthold revealed their true identities as the Armored Titan and the Colossal Titan, respectively. This shocking revelation came after a conversation with Eren, where they both confessed that they were the ones who had attacked humanity in Shiganshina and Trost . Reiner and Berthold 's confession confirmed the suspicions of the Legion, who had been searching for those responsible for the destruction of the walls and the attack of the Titans. The emotional impact of this betrayal was very strong for Eren, as he considered them as older brothers.

Berthold 's betrayal led to a series of conflicts and revelations. During the confrontation, Reiner and Berthold kidnapped Eren and Ymir. This betrayal was a blow to Eren, who could not believe that the people he trusted had betrayed him in such a way. In turn, the Legion discovered that the Beast Titan was an ally of Reiner and Berthold , and that he was responsible for everything that had happened recently. While, on the other hand, the Legion did not lose hope of recovering their comrades.

Ymir's past was revealed, showing her connection to Historia and the reason for her decision to go with Reiner and Berthold . Ymir, in her past, had been worshipped as a goddess before being captured by the military and turned into a Titan. For 60 years she wandered as a Titan, until one day she met Reiner, Annie and Berthold . Because of this, after discovering a strong bond with Historia, she decided to go with the traitors to locate the young woman and take her with her.

The Legion fought tirelessly to rescue Eren and Historia. During the chase, Erwin lured the Titans towards Reiner and Berthold to give the Legion time to advance. In this chase, Erwin was seriously wounded, but continued to give orders to the rest of the Legion to achieve their goal. However, Ymir, despite having the opportunity to live within the walls, decided to join Reiner and Berthold , seeking her own way to redeem herself for the sins of the past. The Legion managed to recover Eren and Historia, but the battle had left many losses, leaving a great sense of uncertainty.

After a series of events, Ymir made the decision to return with Reiner and Berthold . She knew that they would be punished for their failure in the mission, and offered herself as "spoils" so that they could avoid a worse punishment. Her decision was a sacrifice for her bond with Historia, and demonstrated the moral complexity of the characters in this story. On the other hand, the Legion managed to return with Eren to the Trost district and after the recent revelations, they were able to confirm the theory that all Titans were transformed humans.

Eventually, Erwin, after hearing a testimony from Conny, smiled as he realized that they were one step closer to the truth about the Titans. Ymir's sacrifice, the revelations about the Reiss family, and the nature of the Titans, made the Legion realize that the truth was closer than they thought. The hope of discovering the secrets of the outside world and the origins of the Titans became the main motivation for the Legion, preparing them for what was to come next. In turn, Eren, Mikasa , and Armin realized that the battle against the Titans was much more complex than they imagined, and that there were still many mysteries left to be solved.

The Search for Truth and the Fall of the Government

Following the recent events, the Survey Corps became focused on finding the truth about the Titans and the outside world. Eren in particular began practicing using his Titan Power, specifically the Hardening ability, in hopes of being able to seal the gaps in Wall Maria and Wall Shiganshina . Meanwhile, Historia was revealed to be a key figure, due to her connection to the royal family and the secrets of the Walls. Pastor Nick had mentioned that she was an important person in relation to the Walls, which further raised intrigue about her role.

However, the relative calm would not last long, as the government began to show its hostility towards the Legion, ordering their arrest and the capture of Historia and Eren. This action was due to the secrecy held by the walls, and the government's desire to maintain control over information and power. Faced with this threat, the Legion was forced to flee, seeking refuge in the city of Trost , a place where they could use their three-dimensional maneuvering equipment.

In the midst of the chase, the Legion planned a strategy to avoid Historia and Eren's capture. In an attempt to fool the government, Armin and Jin disguised themselves as them and were captured instead. Meanwhile, Liai and Nifa kept watch on the carriage where the real Historia and Eren were. However, at that precise moment, Kenny, an old acquaintance of Liai's , appeared, shot Nifa and began a chase through the city. The appearance of Kenny, a man with experience in assassinations and a squad working for the government, further complicated the situation.

The chase intensified, with Liai taking on Kenny and his squad, while Mikasa and the rest of the Legion joined the fight. Despite their efforts, the Internal Military Police managed to surround them and take Eren and Historia away. This event marked a critical point in the conflict between the Legion and the government, making it clear that the situation was spiraling out of control.

On the other hand, Erwin began to openly question the government, wondering if it was really worth entrusting them with the future of humanity. Meanwhile, the legion, with the help of a merchant and his son, managed to capture two soldiers responsible for the murder of Pastor Nick, among others. During the interrogation, one of the soldiers, Ralph, revealed the truth about the Reiss family, who turned out to be the real royal family and the one responsible for the troubles at the walls. In turn, it was revealed that the Reiss family possessed the power of a titan that allowed them to manipulate people's memories.

Meanwhile, Rod Reiss, Historia's father, revealed his plan to take back the power of the Founding Titan, using a syringe containing the liquid to turn people into Titans. Rod 's plan was to have Historia turn into a Titan and devour Eren in order to regain power, and thus continue his control of the monarchy. However , Erwin's past and thirst for knowledge drove him to defy the government, as when he was a child, his father was killed for revealing contradictions in the official history. These contradictions made him doubt the official version of events, and led him to seek the truth for himself.

Eventually, the Legion, led by Erwin, staged a coup d'état to overthrow the corrupt government and reveal the truth to the people. In turn, they discovered that the government had no interest in saving humanity, but only sought to maintain their power and social position. In this way, the Legion managed to expose the government's farce to the people, who rallied to their cause. The coup d'état was successful, and the Legion managed to arrest the government leaders and reveal the truth about the Reiss family. Following the coup, Historia was proclaimed as the new queen.

The search for truth and the fight against the government had brought the Legion to a crucial point. Now, with a new government and the support of the people, they were one step closer to unraveling the mysteries that surrounded them and facing the true threats that loomed over humanity.

The Battle at the Chapel and the Transformation of Rod Reiss

Following the coup, the Scout Legion focused on retrieving Eren and Historia from the Reiss family's underground chapel held by Rod Reiss and his group. The situation was critical, as Rod Reiss planned to use Historia to regain the power of the Founding Titan. The Legion devised a plan to infiltrate the chapel and rescue them, knowing that time was running out.

Inside the chapel, Eren experienced a connection to memories from the past as he came into contact with Historia. These memories led him to witness the life of Frida Reiss, Historia's half-sister, who always looked after her. However, Frida had also erased Historia's memories of her. Through these memories, Eren also discovered the past of his own father, Grisha Yeager, who had murdered the entire Reiss family five years ago. In his desperation to regain the power of the Founding Titan, Grisha had transformed into a titan and devoured Frida, gaining the power to control the other titans. In addition to this, he crushed Rod Reiss 's children and wife .

Rod Reiss, now obsessed with regaining his family's power, planned to use a syringe of spinal fluid to turn Historia into a Titan, intending for her to devour Eren and gain the power of the Founding Titan. However, Historia, remembering Ymir's words about living with her head held high, decided to rebel against her father. In an act of defiance, she broke the syringe, thus preventing her own transformation and freeing Eren from his chains. However, a desperate Rod Reiss drank the fluid and transformed himself into a colossal-sized Titan, much larger than the Colossal Titan known to date.

Amidst the chaos, the Legion faced Rod Reiss' Titan, while Eren discovered a new power within himself: the Hardening ability, allowing him to protect his comrades and create a cover to prevent the chapel from collapsing. Despite this new power, the Legion found themselves in a difficult situation, as Rod 's Titan was too powerful and had the ability to regenerate.

Rod Reiss ' Titan was to blow up the Titan's mouth with explosives, taking advantage of Eren's new hardening ability. In addition, the Legion had to get the people out of the district, as Rod 's Titan was attracted to large concentrations of people, so if they got the people out the Titan would go straight for the walls. The battle was arduous, but eventually, Historia, with her own hands, managed to end the Titan's neck, defeating her father and ending his threat. After Rod Reiss' death, Historia was recognized as the rightful heir to the throne, solidifying the shift in power within the walls.

The fight in the chapel had not only posed a great challenge to the Legion, but had also revealed crucial secrets about the origin of the Titans and the power of the Reiss family. Furthermore, it demonstrated Historia's determination to forge her own path and not follow her father's wishes. Finally, with the defeat of Rod Reiss, the Legion had managed to recover Eren and Historia, consolidating their position as defenders of humanity, and ushering in a new era, where the truth was beginning to come to light and hope for a better future was beginning to be reborn.

Finally, it should be noted that during this battle in the chapel, Eren experienced memories about his father Grisha , who revealed to him that after killing the Reiss family, he took him to a forest and transformed him into a pure titan with a syringe. Afterwards, he forced him to devour his father in order to pass on to him the power of the titan he originally had and the power he stole from the Reis family. This revelation shocked Eren, making him further question his role in the world and the truth behind history.

The Reign of History and the Discovery of the Ackermans

Following the defeat of Rod Reiss, Historia was crowned as the new queen of Paradis , marking a new chapter in the history of the walls. The people, who had witnessed her bravery in the fight against the Colossal Titan, accepted her as their rightful ruler. Historia, aware of her role and the responsibility that came with the throne, dedicated herself to rebuilding society and ensuring the well-being of all citizens, especially orphaned children and those in need. Her reign marked an era of prosperity and hope, where the people united under her leadership.

However, the battle against Rod Reiss's Titan left deep scars on the Scout Legion. Despite the victory, many soldiers fell in the fight, proving once again the great sacrifices they had to make to protect humanity. Among the survivors, Levi was still dealing with the loss of his comrades and his own internal struggle.

In the midst of this context, the past of Kenny Ackerman, a key character in the recent history of the Legion, was revealed. After being defeated in the chapel, Kenny survived and had a final conversation with Levi, where he gave him a syringe to turn into a titan. In this conversation, Kenny revealed details about his past, such as his encounter with Uri Reiss, the holder of the Founding Titan at the time. Kenny had been captured by Uri, but Uri decided to let him live, despite the fact that Kenny knew the secret of the royal family and that they could not erase his memory for being an Ackerman. In addition, Uri apologized to Kenny for the hatred his clan had suffered throughout history. From that moment on, Kenny decided to work alongside Uri, ending the persecution of the

Ackermans. It was also learned that Kenny was Levi's uncle and that he had taken care of him when he was a child, before abandoning him.

Before he died, Kenny reflected on the meaning of life and why people hold on to different beliefs and goals. Kenny decided not to use the syringe, revealing to Levi that every person he met searched for meaning in their life, whether it was in a god, alcohol, a dream, a child, or power, they all needed something to keep going. With these words, Kenny passed away, leaving behind a complex legacy that deeply impacted Levi.

Following Kenny's death and Historia's ascension to the throne, Levi was faced with a difficult decision. After Erwin's death, Levi had promised to finish off the Beast Titan, but in the end Armin became the Colossal Titan and was no longer the only one who could defeat him. At the same time, Levi understood that the fight did not end with the defeat of Rod 's Titan and that humanity must continue forward despite the losses. Levi decided to honor the memory of his companions and the sacrifice they had made.

Historia, for her part, proved to be a wise and just leader. Her reign was characterized by her social work, helping orphans and the needy, as well as her determination to seek the truth and uncover the secrets of the world. Her legitimacy and popularity made her the ruler Paradis needed to face the challenges ahead.

Historia's reign marked a new era of hope and rebuilding. The discovery of Kenny's past and the death of Rod Reiss ushered in a series of reflections on power, responsibility, and the meaning of life. The Legion, though battered by loss, remained united and ready to face the challenges of the future, guided by a determination to protect humanity and seek the truth. Historia's recognition as queen was a turning point in the history of the walls, cementing a new order and paving the way for the battles to come.

Grisha's Basement

With Historia's reign consolidated, the Scout Legion set out to uncover the truth about the outside world and the mystery of Grisha Yeager's basement. To do so, they must recapture the Shiganshina district, the launching point of the Titan invasion that changed the course of their lives. Before embarking on this crucial mission, the Legion looked to Grisha's past for answers, turning to instructor Keith Shadis, who had met Grisha years before.

Shadis revealed that he found Grisha 20 years ago outside the gate of the Shiganshina district, with no memories of how he had gotten there other than his name and his profession as a doctor. Shadis described him as a mysterious man who, upon learning of the Scout Legion's mission, considered it something special, something reserved only for the chosen ones. Over time, Grisha married Carla, a woman Shadis loved, but who preferred Grisha. Shadis also confessed that, although he became a commander of the Legion, he always felt like a spectator, unable to influence events. After the attack on Wall Maria, Shadis was unable to prevent Grisha from taking Eren to inject him with the Titan Serum. In his account, Shadis admitted that, in the end, he realized that his student Eren was special, just as Grisha had thought of the Legion.

On the other hand, the Legion also had to deal with the consequences of using the syringe that turns people into titans. Levi, after Kenny's death, finally decides to give the syringe to Armin instead of Erwin, who had died in the recent battle against the Beast Titan. Levi made this decision realizing that in that world, Erwin had no choice but to be a demon and that it was time to let him rest. Levi preferred to trust Armin, considering him the true salvation of humanity. With this, Armin devoured Bertolt and obtained the power of the Colossal Titan.

Finally, the Legion was ready to move into the Shiganshina district . After breaking through the basement door of Eren's house, they discovered Grisha's laboratory , filled with medical artifacts and books containing the truth about the outside world. These books revealed the history of the goddess Ymir, the creation of the Titans, and the people of Eldia , who had been persecuted and oppressed for centuries. They also discovered that Grisha had come to the island on a mission to steal the Founding Titan's power, thus becoming a key player in the history of this conflict. The books also showed the story of how a royal woman named Dina Fritz was sent to the island, with whom Grisha had a son named Zick .

Before the crucial operation, the Legion held a final dinner, a time of camaraderie and reflection. During this dinner, Armin and Eren had a meaningful conversation, recalling the day when Armin showed Eren a book about the outside world, sparking his curiosity and yearning for freedom. With renewed hope, the Legion embarked on a mission to recapture the Shiganshina district , where the final battle that would change the fate of humanity would be fought.

Upon reaching the district, the Legion split up to guard the area and block the outer entrance to Shiganshina . Once this was accomplished, they had to block the inner entrance to the district in order to continue advancing, but it was vital to finish off Reiner and Bertolt, who were in the area. During this time, Armin discovered signs of the presence of three people in the district, which gave them the impression that they were nearby. In addition, Erwin suspected that Reiner and Bertolt had seen them arrive much earlier, which meant that they were probably shifting titans. The plan for the reconquest included a great sacrifice, as was already customary for the Scout Legion.

The search for the truth about the outside world and the mystery of Grisha's basement led the Scout Legion to undertake a mission to reconquer the Shiganshina district. The discovery of Grisha's secrets, his relationship with Shadis, and the power of the Syringe led to a series of crucial decisions, marking the fate of the Legion and humanity. Armin and Eren's conversation at the Last Supper reflected their yearning for freedom and hope, which accompanied the Legion to their next encounter with their enemies.

The Battle of Shiganshina and the Death of Erwin

The return to the Shiganshina district marked the beginning of a crucial battle for the Survey Legion, where they would face their most dangerous enemies and the truth that was hidden behind the walls. Armin, with his keen intelligence, had a feeling that the enemy was hiding within the walls themselves. This suspicion led the Legion to inspect the inside of the walls, discovering a hollow space where Reiner was hiding, revealing his presence and transforming into a titan. The situation was further complicated by the appearance of a large number of titans led by the Beast titan, who blocked the entrance to the district to prevent the horses from entering.

Faced with this situation, Erwin made the decision to split the Legion into two groups. The first group, led by Levi, would be in charge of protecting the horses from the small titans. The second group, where Hanji and Eren were, would protect Eren from his enemies. Meanwhile, Eren transformed into a titan to force Reiner to face him, preventing him from attacking the horses and the rest of the legion. Thus began an intense battle between Eren and Reiner, where Eren demonstrated his mastery of the hardening skill. During the confrontation, Reiner's past was remembered, together with Bertolt, on the day that Eren covered the hole in Trost , where it was shown that both had coldly calculated to take Eren if he was in danger. In that memory, they realized that Marco had heard them and therefore silenced him.

Meanwhile, Bertolt launched a surprise attack, dropping from the sky onto Shiganshina , destroying much of the district. In this attack, the Legion suffered heavy losses, but managed to fend them off with the help of Hanji , who survived the explosion and helped the Legion defeat the Colossal Titan.

As the battle intensified, Erwin realized that the situation was becoming increasingly unfavorable for humanity. He remembered his selfishness in prioritizing his dream above everything else, including his comrades and his missions, but at the same time he knew that he could not give up. At this moment, Levi recognizes that it was because of him that the Legion was able to get this far and asks him to give up his dream to die so that he can defeat the Beast Titan. Thus Erwin decides to lead a suicidal attack against the Beast Titan, aiming to create an opportunity for Levi to approach the titan and defeat it. With this decision, Erwin sacrifices himself along with most of his comrades, who followed his order and charged towards the enemy, while Levi manages to reach the Beast Titan.

Levi, consumed by rage and determination, manages to defeat Zeke, but the battle does not end there. The Colossal Titan, Bertolt, had caused great destruction and Eren was exhausted. At this crucial moment, Armin, severely injured, was sacrificed by Levi who used the syringe on him to make him devour Bertolt and gain the power of the Colossal Titan, as he considered him to be the salvation of humanity, and not Erwin. Erwin dies, leaving behind a legacy of sacrifice and leadership.

After the battle, Armin awoke as the new wielder of the Colossal Titan, but shattered by the death of his friend. The Legion, though victorious, suffered irreparable losses. At this point, the Legion delved into Grisha 's basement , where they found the laboratory and books that revealed the truth about the outside world, the history of Eldia , the Titans, and also why Grisha went to the island.

The Battle at Shiganshina was a turning point in the history of humanity within the walls. The revelation of Reiner's plan, the division of the Legion, the sacrifice of Erwin and his comrades, Levi's decision to inject the syringe into Armin instead of Erwin, the defeat of the Titans, and the discovery of the truth about the world, led to a new chapter in the fight for survival and freedom. The Legion, though battered, was ready to face the new challenges ahead, determined to protect humanity and seek the truth. Erwin's death, despite his sacrifice, was a blow to the Survey Legion, but in turn, it gave way to new decisions that would change the fate of humanity.

The Outside World and the History of Humanity

Following the reconquest of Shiganshina District and the discovery of Grisha 's basement , the Survey Legion gained crucial information about the outside world and the true history of humanity. The world map revealed that Paradis Island , where they lived, was only a small part of a much vaster world. Humanity had not gone extinct, but other civilizations existed with different cultures, technologies, and conflicts.

In the basement, the story of Ymir Fritz, a key figure in the origin of the Titans, was also revealed. It was said that Ymir had made a pact to obtain the power of the Titans, and that this power had fragmented into nine, giving rise to different types of Titans. The people of Eldia , descendants of Ymir, had used this power to invade and oppress other peoples, until the people of Marley managed to wrest seven of the nine Titan powers from them, forcing the King of Eldia to flee to Paradis Island .

Marley planned to reclaim the Founding Titan's power from the royal family of Paradis Island. To do so, they recruited Eldian warriors to inherit the Titans' powers and send them to the island to steal the Founding Titan's power. In this context, the past of Grisha Yeager and his family was revealed . It was learned that Grisha , being an Eldian , had lived in Marley and that his sister had died due to mistreatment by the guards. In his quest for revenge, he joined a group of Eldian restorers and infiltrated Paradis with the mission of stealing the Founding Titan's power.

Another important fact was the discovery of the power of the Attack Titan, which has the ability to see the memories of the past and future of its bearers, and with this ability, Grisha influenced his own decisions and in turn, Eren influenced Grisha's decisions. So it was revealed that Grisha had murdered the royal family, except for Historia's father, in order to steal the power of the founding titan and inject the titan serum into his son Eren, so that he could continue his mission to recover the founding titan.

The Founding Titan's power was also revealed to be capable of controlling titans and modifying people's memories, but this power was influenced by the first king, who sought peace within the walls. It was discovered that the first king of the walls, Karl Fritz, took his people to Paradis Island to lock themselves within the walls made of thousands of titans, in order to prevent further wars and oppress humanity, but that if anyone threatened peace, he would take revenge.

After learning all these secrets, Historia, now queen, decides to share the truth with the population, revealing the true history of humanity and the outside world. The leaders of the legion now knew that they must prepare to face a new enemy, no longer just the titans, but also other human civilizations. Eren, possessor of the Attack Titan and the Founding Titan, became a key figure in the future of humanity, as he could use the power of the Founding Titan, but without the influence of the first king, due to not being of royal blood. However, Eren discovered that he could use the power of the Founding Titan to the fullest when he came into contact with a titan of royal blood.

The revelation of the outside world and humanity's history, the story of Ymir Fritz and the origin of the Titans, Marley's plan, and Grisha 's past led the Survey Corps to make new choices in their fight for survival and freedom. The power of the Attack Titan, the influence of the First King, and Eren's role as the bearer of the Founding Titan all became central elements in the future of humanity. Historia's decision to share the truth with the people marked a new chapter in the history of Paradis Island , and laid the groundwork for a new fight for freedom.

The Marley Expedition and the World Alliance

Paradis Island , and after learning the truth of the outside world, Eren longed to see the sea, a dream he had shared with Armin since childhood. However, this desire transformed into a darker determination when he understood the extent of the world's hatred and hostility towards his people. Eren made the decision to infiltrate Marley, the nation that had orchestrated the attack on Shiganshina , in order to understand its enemies and plan a strategy to protect Paradis .

Meanwhile, Marley was preparing for a new war, this time against Paradis Island , following the failure of the mission to recover the Founding Titan. A new Jaw Titan, Porco Galliard , was introduced, brother of the deceased Marcel, who held a grudge against Reiner for not being the one to inherit the Armored Titan. Reiner, in turn, reunited with his family in Liberio, a city where Eldians lived segregated and oppressed by the Marley Empire, and where Eldians were used as soldiers to fight in wars.

In an attempt to unite the world against Paradis Island , Willy Tybur , head of a powerful Eldian family that enjoyed privileges in Marley, held a speech on Liberio. In this speech, Tybur revealed the true history of humanity, debunking Marley's narrative and exposing the plans of the first King Fritz who had created the walls on Paradis Island . However, Tybur accused Eren of being the main threat to the world, revealing his plan to remove King Fritz's war-renouncing pact. With the public on his side, Tybur declared war on Paradis Island , unaware that Eren had infiltrated the public.

Eren's infiltration into Marley was a strategic act to understand his enemy and his plans. During this time, Reiner's past is revealed, who had suffered a dual personality trauma following his mission to Paradis , where he acted with two personalities: one tough and determined and another kind and friendly. Reiner had been manipulated into continuing the mission to Paradis and hiding his faults.

Amidst political tension, the Tybur family arrived in Marley with plans to unite the world against Paradis Island . The plan was to use Willy Tybur as a decoy to lure Eren and the Legion to Liberio and annihilate them, but the Legion and Eren already had a plan. During this event, Eren revealed that his infiltration was intended to destroy Marley's military infrastructure, thus beginning a battle on Liberio.

In the chaos of the battle, the Survey Corps reappeared in Marley, intending to support Eren. The battle on Liberio was brutal and merciless, resulting in the deaths of many Marleyan soldiers and innocent civilians . The Legion, alongside Eren, caused great devastation, demonstrating their power and determination. Amidst the destruction, Eren managed to acquire the power of the War Hammer Titan by devouring its wielder, Lara Tybur . The Colossal Titan, in the hands of Armin, also participated in the battle, causing great destruction to Marley's port.

The expedition to Marley and the World Alliance marked a turning point in the war between Eldia and Marley, where the roles of victims and victimizers blurred, revealing the complexity of the conflict. Eren's desire to see the sea had transformed into a need to protect his people, leading him to make decisions that would put the balance of the world in jeopardy. Marley's preparation for war, Willy Tybur 's speech , Eren's infiltration, and the battle on Liberio were just the beginning of a conflict that would extend beyond the borders of Paradis Island . The reappearance of the Legion in Marley, as well as the sacrifice of the people of Marley, made it clear that hatred and revenge are destructive forces that know no limits.

Zeke's Plan and Euthanasia for the Eldians

Following the attack on Liberio, a new plan emerged as a possible solution to the conflict between Eldia and the rest of the world: Zeke Yeager's plan, which proposed euthanasia for the Eldian people . This plan was based on the idea that the root of suffering and war lay in the existence of the Eldians and their titanic power, so the best option was to prevent their reproduction in order to gradually extinguish their lineage and, with it, the hatred they aroused in the rest of humanity.

Zeke's plan was hatched with the help of a group of anti-Marleyan volunteers , including Yelena , a former Marleyan soldier who had joined Zeke out of her deep conviction that the liberation of the Eldians was the key to a better world. These volunteers presented themselves to the Survey Corps as allies willing to provide information and support for peace, but in reality they were intended to fulfill Zeke's plan, which went far beyond a simple alliance.

Zeke's plan required the activation of the Rumble, the Founding Titan's power capable of unleashing the Colossal Titans that formed the walls of Paradis , and for this, certain requirements needed to be met: the contact of a Titan with royal blood with the power of the Founding Titan. Zeke, as a member of Eldian royalty , offered himself as the key to activate this power, but his true intention was to use the Founding Titan's power to execute euthanasia.

As the Survey Corps prepared for what they believed would be a limited rumble to showcase the island's power, a port was established with the help of the nation of Hizuru , who were interested in Paradis Island , but in reality, were seeking to profit from the situation. The arrival of the country of Hizuru revealed crucial information regarding the connection between Mikasa 's family and the Eldian royalty , raising further questions about Mikasa 's role in the conflict.

In this context, the Founding Titan and royal blood became key points to understanding Zeke's true plan, who not only sought to free the Eldians , but also to eradicate their existence. The power of the Founding Titan was necessary to carry out this plan, so Zeke became a pawn of Eren's goals, who used him for his own purposes. For all this to be possible, it was necessary for a person with royal blood to have the power of the Beast Titan, which would be necessary to use the power of the Founding Titan.

Zeke's plan was jeopardized when Historia, the Queen of Paradis , became pregnant, creating further complications for the euthanasia plan. To ensure the continuation of his plan, Zeke proposed that Historia be turned into a Titan and devour him in order to gain the Beast Titan's power and thus ensure that every generation would have a Titan with royal blood, repeating this process in the future. The Survey Legion opposed this plan, seeing it as a way to turn the Eldians into livestock to ensure world peace, but were unaware of Eren's true plans.

Suspicions about Zeke and Yelena 's true plans led to the arrest of Yelena and the volunteers, while Eren began to act increasingly independently and mysteriously, with the Hammer Titan's ability to break out of his cell at will. The Legion found itself torn between support for Eren and distrust of his true purpose, leading to internal tensions. In the end, the Legion discovered that the reason Zeke was put in a forest was because Historia was pregnant, so the plan was put on hold and everyone was suspected of the recent incident.

Zeke's plan to euthanize the Eldians created a deep divide within the Survey Legion and the population of Paradis . While some saw this plan as a way to end the cycle of hatred, others resisted the idea of extinguishing their own bloodline, bringing the Legion to a breaking point and questioning the future of humanity. The decisions they would make from then on would have a decisive impact on the fate of Eldia and the world. Eren, in turn, already had his own plan in mind, and Zeke and the Legion's actions would be a catalyst for what was to come in the future. The Founding Titan and the Rumble were more than just a means, they were the key to their plan of annihilation.

Eren's Internal Conflict and Betrayal

Following the spread of the truth about the outside world and Zeke's euthanasia plan, internal conflict began to brew on Paradis, where distrust and uncertainty took hold within the Survey Corps. The Jaegerists, a group of soldiers loyal to Eren, took control of the situation, spreading their ideology of Eldian supremacy and exerting pressure on the rest of the population, including his former comrades. This group sought the total annihilation of humanity outside the walls, and believed that Eren was the leader who would lead them to victory, even if it meant sacrificing innocent lives.

Meanwhile, Marley prepared for a counterattack on Paradis, intending to reclaim the Founding Titan's power and annihilate the Legion. However, distrust of Eren deepened, even among his own friends and fellow Legion members. Eren's decision-making without consulting anyone, and his mysterious change of heart regarding Zeke's plan, raised questions about his true loyalties and intentions. Finding Zeke became a priority, as he was believed to be the only one who could stop Eren's plans.

In the midst of this climate of tension, the capture of the restaurant where Nicolo worked, a Marleyan soldier who had become fond of Sasha, revealed a new piece in the puzzle. The wine that Nicolo had served to the Eldians contained Zeke's bone marrow fluid, a powerful agent that would allow Zeke to control those who ingested it, turning them into titans at his will. This fact, coupled with the recent explosion at Nile's office, revealed a new piece in the puzzle. Dok generated even more distrust towards Eren and his followers.

The situation came to a head when Eren directly confronted Armin, Mikasa , and Gabi, his former classmates. In this confrontation, Eren revealed his belief in individual freedom and his decision to follow his own path, no matter the consequences. Eren criticized Armin for living in Bertolt's memories, and Mikasa for her dependence on him, making it clear that he was not the same boy they knew, as he now saw time in a different way, being able to see the past, present, and future at the same time. This confrontation made it clear that Eren was willing to sacrifice everything for his ideal of freedom, including his friends and the rest of the world.

The workings of Zeke's bone marrow fluid proved to be one of the most dangerous weapons in this conflict. Zeke could control all Eldians who had ingested this fluid, turning them into pure Titans by simply shouting, leaving them without any control over their own bodies. This ability of Zeke's, coupled with the Jaegerists ' control of Paradis , led to an even more chaotic and desperate situation, where no one seemed to be sure which path to take.

Faced with this situation, Levi, who had already distrusted Zeke since his arrival, made the decision to act on his own. Levi proposed sacrificing Zeke, as he considered him the root of all the problems. However, this plan was thwarted when Zeke managed to flee, leaving Levi and his men with no escape route. At this point, the situation was becoming increasingly confusing and dangerous for everyone, where every decision could be the last and the boundaries of morality and loyalty were blurred in the face of the growing darkness.

In this bleak panorama, Eren's betrayal was not only an act of rebellion, but a symptom of the deep crisis that the world was experiencing, where hatred, fear and despair seemed to be the only forces guiding the decisions of human beings. The fight for freedom and peace had transformed into a pitched battle for survival, where sacrifice and death had become the order of the day.

Zeke's Past and His Connection to the Founding Titan

The past of Zeke, a key character in the conflict, reveals a story marked by the influence of his parents and his training as a warrior. Since childhood, Zeke was subjected to a rigorous regime to become a warrior of Marley, where he was instilled with the idea that Eldians were inferior beings and deserved to be punished. However, his parents, restorers of Eldia , passed on to him the true history of their people, contradicting Marley's version. This duality in his education generated an internal conflict in Zeke, who always strove to excel in his training to earn Marley's recognition, but without leaving aside his Eldian roots . Despite being considered the worst of his group, Zeke always looked for a way to be useful, both to his people and to Marley, no matter what he had to do to achieve it.

Eldian euthanasia . Influenced by Xaver , the previous owner of the Beast Titan, Zeke believed that the only way to end the hatred towards the Eldians was to prevent them from reproducing. Xaver , a man marked by personal tragedy, revealed to Zeke that this was the only solution to his suffering and that there was no other way to find peace in this world. Zeke adopted this plan as a personal mission, convinced that it was the only way to free his people from the cycle of hatred and suffering. In this way, and with the conviction of doing the right thing, Zeke decides to take this path, where as cruel as it may seem, it was his way to free the world from all the evil that surrounded it.

Consequently, Zeke's plan was to use the Founding Titan's power to euthanize the Eldians . To do so, he needed to contact Eren, the Founding Titan's wielder, and convince him that his plan was the right path. Zeke presented himself as an ally to Eren, but he actually saw him as a tool to fulfill his goal of "liberating" the world from the Eldians . This duality of Zeke's, between his desire to save his people and his radical euthanasia plan, generated great tension and distrust in those who knew him. The power of the Beast Titan, coupled with his ability to turn other Eldians into pure Titans, made him one of the greatest threats in the conflict.

Zeke's anger, fueled by the suffering of his people and Marley's manipulation, manifested itself in his determination to carry out his plan for euthanasia. His obsession with the baseball, an object that represented his desire to return to his childhood, was a sign of his deep despair and his longing for a world without hatred and war. This baseball becomes the symbol of his own life, where he only repeated the same pattern without finding any true meaning. In the midst of war, Zeke only seeks to return to the safety and peace of his childhood, when he did not have the pressure of saving the world or deciding who should live or die.

Despite his radical plan, Zeke had to make difficult decisions that led him to betray his own allies. After manipulating Levi and his squad, he escaped from his confinement, leaving behind his own comrades turned into Titans. However, this act of betrayal allowed him to meet up with Eren and carry out his plan to use the power of the Founding Titan. Levi, for his part, felt betrayed and swore revenge against Zeke, who had become an even more dangerous enemy than before. At that moment, Levi only had the goal of killing Zeke in mind, not caring about anything else.

Eldians connect through the Founding Titan, and had an encounter with Ymir, the founder of the Titans' power. In this encounter, Zeke believed that Ymir would fulfill his will to euthanize him, but was surprised by Ymir's decision to follow Eren. This unexpected turn of events left Zeke with no options, and confirmed that the Founding Titan's true power lay in Ymir's will, a will that had remained chained to King Fritz for over 2000 years. In the Paths, Zeke was able to see his past, present, and future at the same time, where he even had one last conversation with Armin, demonstrating a small change in his way of thinking, but it was too late to turn back.

Zeke's past, his training as a warrior, his influence at the hands of his parents, and his relationship with Xaver are key elements in understanding his motivations and his connection to the Founding Titan. His plan to euthanize him, his anger, and his decision to betray Levi and his companions are the result of a life marked by hatred, despair, and the desire to change the world in his own way. His encounter with Ymir on the Roads led him to understand that the Founding Titan's power lies in the Founder's will, not his own, which led to his defeat.

In this context, Zeke's figure rises as that of a complex antagonist, a man who fought for his ideals, but whose decisions led him to cause even more pain and suffering, where his past and his obsession were one of the main reasons for the destruction and tragedy of many.

The Activation of the Rumble and Eren's True Will

The arrival in Shiganshina marked a crucial point in the conflict, where the plan to recover the Founding Titan and the truth about Eren's intentions began to be revealed. Amidst the desolation and memories of the fall of Wall Maria, Eren, along with the Scout Legion, prepared to face Reiner, Porco, and the other warriors of Marley. However, the true battle would not only be on the physical plane, but on the plane of ideas and will, where the plans of each side would collide in an event that would change the world forever. The fight in Shiganshina was the stage where all of Eren's power and the magnitude of his determination for a future that he himself planned were unleashed.

In the midst of the confrontation, Eren faced Reiner and Porco, demonstrating a superior mastery of his powers as a Titan. Eren did not hesitate to use his abilities to fight back, while the enemy tried to stop him at all costs. Despite the intensity of the fight, the true threat lay in Zeke's strategy, who waited for his moment to activate his plan. At a critical moment, Zeke screamed, transforming nearby soldiers into pure Titans and demonstrating the extent of his power. The situation became even more desperate when the alliance between Eren and Zeke seemed to be the catalyst for a new era of chaos and destruction.

The activation of the Rumble marked a turning point in the conflict. Eren, after coming into contact with Zeke, managed to access the power of the Founding Titan, unleashing thousands of Colossal Titans that were within the walls. This catastrophic event not only posed a threat to the outside world, but also revealed Eren's true will and his determination to protect the people of Paradis at all costs. With this plan, Eren did not seek the liberation of the Eldians, but their safety through the annihilation of all their enemies. The magnitude of the Founding Titan's power was evident, and with it, the gulf between Eren and his allies seemed to grow with each moment.

However, Eren's actions were not the result of a momentary impulse, but part of a carefully calculated plan. In a trip through Grisha's memories, Zeke and Eren discovered that Eren had manipulated his own father through the power of the Attack Titan. This titan has the ability to see the past and future of all of its wielders, allowing Eren to manipulate the past to create the future he desired. In this way, every event, every decision of the characters, was influenced by the Attack Titan, proving that Eren was always one step ahead of everyone.

Eren, using this power, modified his father's actions so that he would transmit the power of the Founding Titan to him, kill the Reiss family and thus guide the Legion towards the truth that was in the basement of his house. In other words, all the events that led to the present were caused by Eren himself, where he manipulated the past to forge a future where he would be able to unleash his power. This showed that Eren's intention was none other than to achieve the power necessary to achieve his goal of exterminating his enemies. With this, Eren's figure changed before everyone's eyes, going from being a symbol of hope to an entity of total destruction.

Eren's manipulation of Grisha and his control over the past revealed the extent of the Attack Titan's power and Eren's determination. His ability to influence events and the decisions of others allowed him to orchestrate a plan that would lead him to achieve his goal. Eren became a manipulator of history, an architect of fate who had sacrificed his own freedom to protect his people. As the truth was revealed, everyone's image of Eren crumbled before their very eyes, making their own decisions seem pointless.

The truth about Eren showed that his fight was not just against the Titans, but against destiny itself. His control over the past and the future allowed him to make decisions that, although terrible, were guided by his deep conviction that they were necessary to save the island of Paradis . The truth showed that every decision, every death and every event, were part of Eren's plan, where everything and everyone were pieces of his own strategy. With all this, the figure of Eren became that of a superior being with absolute power, but also with the weight of all the consequences of his decisions.

In this context, Ymir's connection to Eren's will took on a new dimension. Ymir, the founder of the Titans' power, had been chained to King Fritz's will for centuries, but it was Eren who offered her freedom and the chance to decide her own destiny. This connection between Eren and Ymir allowed the Rumble to take place, freeing the founder's will and proving that her loyalty was not to the King, but to Eren. With all this, Eren's plan was shown to be an inevitable event, where even the founder's will had been manipulated by her own strategy.

Ultimately, the sacrifice of humanity for the freedom of Paradis became the culmination of Eren's plan. His determination to protect his people led him to make extreme decisions, such as activating the Rumble and destroying much of the world. Despite the dire consequences of his actions, Eren believed that it was the only way to ensure the survival of Paradis and break the cycle of hatred and revenge that had plagued his people. Thus, Eren decided to become the enemy of the world, despite the pain it caused all of his comrades, with the conviction that at least, in this way, the people he loved would live in peace.

The activation of the Rumble and the revelation of Eren's true will were momentous events that changed the course of the conflict. His manipulation of the past, his connection to Ymir, and his determination to protect his people at all costs made him a controversial and complex character, a titan who was able to control history to bring about a future where his people could live in freedom, even if it meant the death of most people. His plan, though terrible, was executed with a precision and determination that demonstrated the magnitude of his power and the depth of his convictions, even if it meant the total destruction of the world.

In this way, Eren becomes a symbol of human complexity, a character whose decisions, although marked by desperation, also demonstrated a strength of will and determination that made him one of the most important characters in this conflict, making it clear that no matter how cruel it may seem, he would do whatever it takes to achieve the goal he set for himself.

The Final Fight and the Legacy of the Legion

The final fight was triggered by Connie's determination and Falco's sacrifice, marking a turning point in the war. Connie, consumed by the desire to save his mother, took Falco with the intention of having his mother's titan devour him and regain his human form. This desperate action, however, would be the trigger for a series of events that would lead the alliance to seek a definitive solution. Connie's desperation contrasted with Falco's will, who, despite the danger, would become a key piece for the destiny of all. In this moment of chaos, hope seemed lost, but the alliance would not give up.

Amidst the confusion, Armin, having witnessed the magnitude of the rumble and the consequences of the war, desperately searched for a solution to stop Eren. The pressure of being a leader and having to make decisions, brought him to a point of reflection where he confessed to being a monster, just like Annie, acknowledging the weight of his own actions and the sacrifices he had made. Armin not only blamed himself for the current situation, but also for the actions of the past that had led him to this point, including his decision to survive instead of Erwin. In his search for answers, he realized that there were no heroes or villains, only people who fought for their convictions and who had to stop Eren at all costs.

Meanwhile, Floch was establishing himself as a leader of the Jaegerists , enforcing his control over the island and eliminating anyone who opposed his vision. Floch 's betrayal showed that the division between the island's inhabitants was still simmering, and that the conflict was not only being waged against the outside, but also within their own ranks. With this, the Jaegerists became an enemy to both the alliance and the world, and their control over the island made the situation increasingly complicated. Floch's fanaticism blinded the rest, causing chaos on the island and making the alliance the only hope for the world.

However, the alliance was not willing to fight alone, and in an unexpected turn, Magath and Pieck offered their support to stop Eren. Magath, recognizing the cruelty of his own nation, apologized to the legion, making it clear that the last thing he wanted was for the world to be destroyed by Eren's decisions. Thus, Magath and Pieck joined the cause, and together, they would plan the strategy to stop Eren, putting aside their differences and focusing on the common goal of saving the world from destruction. The union of the alliance was the only hope to stop the rumble, but the situation looked very complicated.

Amidst the growing tension, Falco demonstrated the potential of his newfound power as a Titan. Thanks to the properties of his Titan, which combined the characteristics of the Jaw Titan and the Beast, Falco gained the ability to fly. This ability was crucial to the alliance, as it allowed them to move quickly and overcome obstacles that previously seemed impossible, being a catalyst for the group's decisions. Falco, as just a child, assumed a very important role in the future of the world, marking a key point in the fight for humanity. In this way, Falco and his Titan became a symbol of hope.

The attack on the World Fleet and the arrival at Fort Salta marked a turning point in the war. The alliance was preparing to face Eren, but the difficulties would be too much. Eren, using the power of the Founding Titan, caused great damage, but also caused the alliance to not give up, having a common goal: to stop Eren. The alliance, despite their differences, would fight to the end to save humanity, even if it meant fighting their own comrades. The situation was very complicated, but the alliance group was not willing to give up.

While all this was going on, the alliance's decision was centered on the desire to kill Zeke, who was the key to activating the Founding Titan's power. The members of the alliance not only wanted to stop Zeke, but their hatred for him increased with each new action of the enemy, making them think that the only way to end the war was to kill him. Zeke's death, although necessary, represented the loss of a key piece for the alliance, since Zeke had been playing a very important role in the conflict. The members of the alliance doubted their future, but the decision was made: it was necessary to kill Zeke in order to stop Eren.

Finally, at the most critical point of the war, Eren communicated with the alliance through the paths, explaining his true intentions. In this dialogue with the alliance, Eren not only confessed to them that his intention was to end the world, but also explained to them that he had always wanted them to stop him, making them become the heroes that the world needed. In this way, Eren's plan was revealed in all its magnitude, demonstrating that there was no freedom, but the inevitability of destiny. Eren's dialogue with his companions showed that the entire plan was nothing more than a selfish act, with which he sought a path where his people could live in peace, even if that meant the death of the entire world.

At this point, Eren was not just an enemy, but the embodiment of desperation and sacrifice, willing to do whatever it took to protect his people. The final decision lay with the alliance, who had to stop Eren, even if it meant ending the life of the friend they loved so much. The final fight would be fought on the battlefield, but also in the hearts of each of the characters, who had to decide what was truly worth it.

The final fight represented the point of convergence of all the conflicts, where each character had to make a decision that would change the fate of the world. Connie's decision, Falco's sacrifice, Armin's confession, the agreement with Magath and Pieck , the properties of Falco's titan, and Eren's dialogue with the alliance, were events that marked the end of the story. In this way, the world would be involved in an unprecedented battle, where the alliance had to fight against the most powerful being in the world, their former friend. The final fight showed that there was no good or evil, but that the decisions of each individual were what really mattered in building the world.

Ymir's Connection to Eren's Will

The connection between Ymir and Eren's will was revealed to be the linchpin of the final fight, a force that transcended time and space. Eren, understanding Ymir's millennia-long enslavement as the Founding Titan , and her yearning for freedom, became the catalyst for her liberation, driving her to make her own choices after 2,000 years of serving the royal lineage. Ymir, recognizing in Eren a genuine desire for freedom, chose to follow his will, allowing the Rumble to be unleashed and the power of the Titans to fade away, proving that the connection between the two was so strong, it was able to manifest throughout history. This connection not only changed the course of the war, but also revealed the true nature of will, proving that it can manifest in many different ways.

In the midst of the conflict, Falco's Titan power manifested itself in a new ability that shocked everyone. Falco, through the combination of the Jaw Titan's power with the Beast Titan's fluid, gained the ability to fly, a power reminiscent of birds. Not only was this ability crucial in saving the alliance on several occasions, but it also revealed the potential of Titan transformations, proving that Titans' abilities could transcend conventional abilities. Falco's Titan proved that even in the midst of war, there was a possibility of hope, and that humanity could still use Titan powers to their own advantage.

Meanwhile, Armin, after being devoured by Ymir, experienced a deep connection with her on the paths, where she revealed to him the origin of life. In this timeless space, Armin discovered that life was a phenomenon that sought to multiply, adapt to all environments and transcend the limitations of existence. However, Armin wondered why Ymir, with such power, had remained a slave for so long, to which she never answered. In this dialogue, Armin also discovered the importance of every little moment, whether it was reading a book, or running with his friends towards the hill. This revelation was crucial for Armin to find the motivation necessary to continue fighting for the future of humanity, and to make it clear that life was not just a mere process of reproduction, but was also based on personal experiences.

In a moment of desperation, the former bearers of the Nine Shifting Titans answered Ymir's call, helping the alliance fight Eren. The specters of Bertolt, Porco, Marcel, Ymir, Xavier, Grisha , and Kruger joined the fight, proving that the Titans' connection transcended death and that the past was always present. The help of the former bearers was crucial to the alliance's ability to confront Eren, but it was also a demonstration that the war was not only a conflict between the present, but also a fight between the past and the future. In this way, the legacy of the Titans became an ally of humanity.

With all this at stake, Levi, fulfilling the promise he made to Erwin before he died, decided to take down Zeke, who had been pulling the strings of the war. Levi, with his unwavering determination, faced Zeke, determined to keep his promise, no matter what it meant. Zeke's death represented a turning point in the war, and showed the world that even though Eren's will was very strong, there would always be someone willing to fight against it. After Zeke's death, Levi felt a bittersweet feeling, as even though he kept his promise, he knew that nothing he had done would change the past.

Despite all the alliance's efforts, Eren's sacrifice became a necessary step towards the Titans' demise. Eren's decision, although drastic, represented an act of love and sacrifice for his friends and for humanity, as his intention was always for the world to stop fighting and for his people to be able to live in peace. The disappearance of the Titans marked the end of an era of oppression and war, but it also represented an uncertain future for humanity, as it would now have no way to defend itself from any threats that might come. The disappearance of the Titans represented the end of a cycle of hatred and revenge, giving way to a new era, where hope would be the only thing left for humanity.

After the final battle, Mikasa , with Eren's head in her hands, said goodbye to him for the last time under the tree where they used to rest. At that moment, a bird arranged the scarf that Eren had given her, creating a moment that connected both of their past, present, and future. This act was a symbol of their unconditional love, and represented Mikasa's way of freeing Eren from his burden, allowing him to rest in peace. Likewise, Ymir, seeing Mikasa's love , realized that she too deserved to be free, and thus, the power of the Titans disappeared from the world. Ymir's liberation was the final point of the story, where her pain and suffering became a catalyst for the end of the wars and the disappearance of the power of the Titans.

Finally, in a space outside of time, Eren and Armin had their last conversation, where they said goodbye. Eren confessed to Armin that his plan to attack the world and force them to kill him was just a way to achieve freedom. In turn, Eren revealed to Armin that his actions were always selfish, since his only goal was always to protect his friends, even if this meant the death of the entire world. In this way, Eren accepted his destiny and gave his friends the opportunity to be the heroes that the world needed. In this final conversation, Eren and Armin reconciled, but not as friends, but as people who, despite their differences, had always understood each other. In this way, Eren said goodbye to his friend, letting him follow a new path in his life, while he prepared for his eternal rest.

The final fight represented the end of a long journey for the characters, where each of them had to make decisions that would change the course of history. Ymir's connection to Eren's will, the power of Falco's Titan, Armin and Ymir's connection, the awakening of the ancient bearers, Levi's decision, Eren's sacrifice, Mikasa 's final goodbye , and Eren and Armin's final conversation, were events that marked the end of the Titans' power and the beginning of a new era for humanity.

Epilogue

After the storm of war and the fading of the Titans' power, a new world began to emerge, marked by the search for peace and reconstruction. Nations devastated by the Rumble were forced to rethink their beliefs and seek a path to reconciliation. Against this backdrop, survivors from both Paradis and the rest of the world worked to heal the wounds of the past and build a future where hatred and vengeance would no longer exist. The task was arduous, but the hope for a new beginning drove humanity forward.

On Paradis , an army was formed to deal with any threat that might arise from outside, aware that peace was a fragile goal and that vigilance was essential. However, the main focus of the island's inhabitants shifted to rebuilding and finding new ways to live peacefully. Queen Historia, along with a council of leaders, dedicated herself to helping the population, especially orphans and the needy, who were the most affected by the war. Reconstruction efforts were not limited to the island, but extended to other territories devastated by the Rumble, demonstrating Paradis ' commitment to a more just world.

Meanwhile, across the rest of the world, nations struggled to put their hatred of the Eldians behind them and seek new ways of cooperation and understanding. Leaders such as Armin, Mikasa , Jean, Conny, Pieck , and Annie returned to Paradis as ambassadors in peace negotiations, seeking to build bridges between nations and prevent past conflicts from happening again. These ambassadors represented hope for a better world, but they also embodied the legacy of those who gave their lives in the fight against the Titans. The efforts of these ambassadors caused nations to begin to rethink the meaning of peace, but they knew that there were those willing to change everything.

Despite efforts to build a better future, Eren's legacy, both as a destroyer and a liberator, became a constant debate among humanity. Some saw him as a monster, responsible for the deaths of millions, while others considered him a hero, who sacrificed himself to save his people and free Ymir. However, everyone agreed that his actions had changed the course of history and left an indelible mark on the world. The debate over Eren's legacy caused the world to begin to rethink the nature of freedom, the meaning of justice, and the lengths to which people were willing to go to achieve their ideals.

In the midst of uncertainty, hope for the future was embodied in the children, who were born into a world without titans, but with the responsibility of building a better future. In these children, there was a longing for a more peaceful and just world, a world where history would not repeat itself and where the mistakes of the past could serve as lessons for the future. Hope was not only found in the children, but also in all the people who, inspired by the sacrifices of the past, decided to fight for a better future.

However, peace was still a distant dream. In Paradis , the military remained vigilant, aware that conflict was inevitable, and that the fight for peace would never end. In the rest of the world, tensions remained simmering, and the risk of new conflicts was always present. The conflicts made people begin to question whether one day, the world could become a peaceful place, without the need for war. Despite everything, humanity, driven by Eren's legacy and hope for the future, continued to search for the path to peace, knowing that the road was long and difficult, but that the effort was worth it.

Mikasa, for her part, lived her final years remembering Eren under the tree where they used to rest together. Her love for him transcended death, and his memory accompanied her until the end of her days. When she died, her legacy joined Eren's, creating a story that would be remembered for generations. Mikasa's love was the demonstration that, in a world where hatred and revenge were the most common, love was always going to be the answer, but also the demonstration that feelings are a force capable of changing the course of things.

Mikasa's death, time continued its march, civilization increased its technology and more wars and conflicts occurred that ended up destroying the lands. In the ruins of the world, someone found the tree where Eren was buried, also finding the remains of his grave. The tree, as a symbol of hope and memory, represented the end of one cycle and the beginning of another, where each person would have the opportunity to build a new future with their own hands. The story of Eren and all his friends remained as a lesson for humanity, a reminder of the importance of peace, love and freedom. The world, after the disappearance of the titans, was forced to rethink its own existence, but above all, learn from its past to build a better future.

The epilogue of this story was not an ending, but a new beginning. The new world, though marked by the scars of the past, embarked on a journey full of challenges and hopes. The search for peace, Eren's legacy, and hope for the future became the pillars of a new era, where humanity had the opportunity to write its own destiny. Peace was the ultimate goal, but along the way, humanity had to learn from its mistakes, forgive its enemies, and fight to make the world it so desired a reality.

Final Note

The quest for freedom is the main driving force of the story. From the beginning, we see Eren's longing to know the outside world and his rejection of conformity within the walls, which leads him to join the Survey Corps. This desire is shared by Armin, who also dreams of exploration and knowledge. The fight for freedom manifests itself in opposition to the Titans, the oppressive walls, and the social structures that limit the characters.

The mystery of the Titans is a key element in the plot. Initially seen as monsters without reason, the story reveals that the Titans are actually transformed humans. The main characters discover that some people can transform into Titans and that the origin of this power is related to the story of Ymir Fritz and the pact with the "demon". The power of the Founding Titan, possessed by Eren, is the most coveted and powerful, capable of controlling other Titans.

The Scout Legion, despite being a force of hope, suffers heavy losses in their fight against the Titans. Scouting missions are extremely dangerous and soldiers must be prepared to sacrifice their lives for humanity. Despite this, camaraderie and a sense of belonging are fundamental aspects for the characters, as seen in the friendship between Eren, Mikasa , and Armin.

The truth about the outside world is far more complex than they imagined. Not only are there other nations, but the Titans themselves are the result of an ancient conflict and a long history of oppression and prejudice. It is revealed that the people of Marley regard the Eldians as demons and use the power of the Titans for their own purposes. This discovery disturbs the protagonists' initial notions and reveals a more complex and ruthless world.

Individual decisions have a huge impact on the plot. Eren's choices to join the Legion, Mikasa's commitment to protecting him, Armin's determination, and Reiner's betrayal are all examples of how each person's actions affect the course of the story. Individual responsibility and the burden of decisions are recurring themes.

The characters display a complex duality. Many characters, both "heroes" and "villains," have internal conflicts and act in unexpected ways. Reiner and Annie are clear examples of individuals who are initially presented as enemies, but are later revealed to have their own complex histories and motivations.

The cycle of hatred and revenge is a constant element. The death of important characters, betrayal, and the desire for revenge fuel the plot. Eren's final decision to activate "The Rumble" is an act of vengeance that threatens to destroy the world.

The end of the story shows a struggle to break the cycle of hatred, albeit at a great cost. Armin's sacrifice and the alliance of different factions aim to stop "The Rumble" and although they succeed, this causes the death of many important characters, the destruction of the power of the Titans and much desolation. In the end, it is shown that peace is possible, but it is not an easy path, and future generations will have to work to prevent the mistakes of the past from being repeated.

Shingeki no Kyojin explores the complexity of the human condition, the struggle for freedom and peace, the impact of war and the power of sacrifice, all against a backdrop of mystery and revelation. It is a story that invites you to reflect on the nature of truth and individual responsibility.

Curiosities

"The creator of the series, Hajime Isayama 's favorite character is Jean Kirstein . Isayama admires her free spirit and the way she speaks her mind without worrying about what others think.

-

"The first season of Attack on Titan aired in Japan in 2013."

-

Hange Zoë 's gender is ambiguous in the manga, and Isayama has stated that he leaves it up to the reader's interpretation. In the translation, specific pronouns were removed to maintain this ambiguity."

-

Hange 's second-in-command and also her assistant. He's also the heaviest drinker on the recon team."

-

"Levi Ackerman is the most popular character in Attack on Titan. on Titan, ranking first in two popularity polls. Eren Jaeger is the second most popular."

-

"Eren's titan form is based on Yushin 's physique Okami a Japanese mixed martial artist."

-

"In 2015, Universal Studios Japan installed an Attack attraction on Titan with life-size titans, including a head of the titan that ate Eren's mother. This attraction was later removed."

-

"At Universal Studios Japan, reconnaissance patrol food portions were offered, with different menus for leaders and regular soldiers."

-

"Originally, it was planned to be known from the beginning that Eren was a titan, but Isayama scrapped the idea."

-

"Eren uses the suffix "-yuki" instead of "-tai " when talking about the titans, thus showing his contempt for them."

-

"Eren's Titan form has eyelid-like membranes, similar to those of some predatory species."

-

" Mikasa doesn't wear her scarf if it's too hot, according to Isayama."

-

"The name Mikasa comes from a battleship of the Imperial Japanese Navy, reflecting the author's interest in female characters named after warships."

-

" Mikasa literally translates as 'three bamboos'."

-

"In an episode of The Simpsons, Lisa appears dressed as Mikasa and using the 3D maneuvering equipment."

-

"Armin Arlert is voiced by voice actress Marina Inoue ."

-

"Marina Inoue also serves as the voice of the series' narrator."

-

"Armin's birthday is on November 3rd, a date that is celebrated in Japan as Culture Day."

-

"Initially, Isayama joked that Armin was the girl Mikasa got along with best, but later clarified that Armin is a boy."

-

"Levi's subordinates refer to him as " Heicho ," which translates to "leader of the soldiers.""

-

"Levi's actual position in the reconnaissance patrol is unusual within the chain of command."

-

"Levi's name was taken from the American documentary ' Jesus Camp'."

-

"The name Levi is of Hebrew origin and means 'attached' or 'to join'."

-

" Isayama has said that Levi is surprisingly old, but he doesn't reveal his exact age, only that he is over 30."

-

"Levi is a tea lover and enjoys collecting tea leaves and brewing it."

-

"The giants became the main theme of Attack on Titan because they are somewhat grotesque."

-

"Humanity's strongest soldier, Levi, can control his drinking and doesn't get drunk."

-

"Levi usually takes quick three-minute baths."

-

"Levi sleeps between 2 and 3 hours a day."

-

"Lack of sleep could explain Levi's height, which is 1.60 meters."

-

"Levi's birthday is on December 25th, and there's a titan who looks a lot like Santa Claus."

-

"Aspects of Levi's design and personality are inspired by Rorschach from Watchmen."

-

"Traits of Ozymandias from Watchmen were used for some of Erwin's features."

-

"Erwin Rommel, known as the Desert Fox, was a source of inspiration for Erwin, including the date of his deaths on October 14."

-

"In Japanese, Erwin's title is " Danchou ", which translates to 'commander'."

-

"Fans joke about Erwin's thick eyebrows, and Erwin's childhood nickname was 'Eyebrow.'"

-

"Erwin remains single because he doesn't know when he will die."

-

"Mike is older than Erwin."

"Mike Zacharias is the tallest human character in the series, standing at six feet tall."

"Mike has a habit of greeting new people by smelling them."

" Isayama received a strange call from his bank due to the sudden increase in funds in his accounts after the success of the series."

"In the anime's intro , there's a soldier riding around in a three-dimensional maneuvering gear that was supposed to be an anonymous representation of humanity, but fans identified it as Dying ."

"The production staff had Dying 's character perform the same maneuver when he encountered the titan."

"Attack on Titan is one of many anime shows banned in China for promoting violence and terrorist activities."

"The first line of the Attack intro " Titan in German is often misunderstood due to inaccurate pronunciation."

-

"Levi appeared in the movie Abduction to focus more on the relationship between Eren and Mikasa ."

-

"In the manga, Annie's uniform when she is confronted as the Female Titan mistakenly has the Recon Patrol symbol on it."

-

"A continuity error in the manga led to theorizing that Reiner was a titan shifter because his previously bitten arm reappeared in a later scene."

-

"Eren's mom's voice was done by Yoshino Takamori , who also played Trisha Elric in Fullmetal Alchemist Alchemist , both mothers of the protagonists with a similar hairstyle."

-

"Isayama is a fan of the Japanese group Linkedin Horizon and listens to them to cheer himself up when drawing sad scenes."

Legal Notice and Copyright

Copyright © 2025 Editorial Nova. All rights reserved.

This book and its contents, including text, images, design, graphics and any other material, are protected by applicable intellectual property and copyright laws.

The reproduction, distribution, modification, transmission, exhibition or any other total or partial use of this material is strictly prohibited without the express written authorization of Editorial Nova.

Exceptions permitted by law, such as personal and non-commercial use, quotation for educational or review purposes, must always include the corresponding acknowledgment to the publisher and author.

Disclaimer

The information contained in this publication is for informational and/or educational purposes. Although every effort has been made to ensure that it is accurate and up-to-date, neither the author nor Editorial Nova assumes responsibility for misinterpretations, decisions or actions taken based on the contents of the book.

If this material contains references to actual brands, products, persons or events, these are included for illustrative purposes only and do not imply any affiliation, endorsement or legal relationship with Editorial Nova.

nova

www.ingramcontent.com/pod-product-compliance
Lightning Source LLC
LaVergne TN
LVHW012033060526
838201LV00061B/4574